Unconditional

Just Me and My Scattered Thoughts

Always,
T. Renee

T. RENEE

Dedication

I am eternally grateful to my Mother, whose love, joy, friendship and compassion are without limit or condition. I could never have written a thing without her faith in me.

To my family… Dumpson, Basnight, Bohanon & Robinson dead and living alike, I am so proud to be related to you all, to have been given the opportunity to know you, love you and be inspired by you. I couldn't imagine my life without you all in it.

To my readers, my friends who've become family and to the admirers I will never meet, thank you for your support. This collection, its content and its title come from my sincere belief that the most important things in life, the best things—are always Unconditional; faith, love, hope and praise… I wish these things for all of you in abundance.

Contents

Life

Let History Teach You Something

Not everything was wrong
not everything was bad,
the past has brought us thus this far
ignoring it will set us back.
Repetition can be dangerous
ambivalence even greater so,
such perilousness of the times we're in
arrogance has left us all exposed.

We've bargained our integrity
We've sold our sense of worth.
We've burned the villages raising children
We've auctioned off the church.
We've sued our way to happiness
We've jailed liberty and truth.
We've martyred accountability
We've placed conjecture in priority above proof.

Remember Independence Day
Remember Armstrong's walk on the moon.
Remember the March on Washington
Remember World War Two.

Don't forget what others gave
Don't forget their sacrifice.
Don't forget their collective efforts
To give the future they'd never see a better life.

By and By

I want you to see
Martin's Dream.
I want you to hear
those four little black girls scream.
I want your flesh to feel
those Dobermans' teeth.
I want your feet to hit the pavement
'cause I'm not giving up my seat.

I want you to attend a segregated facility
where rats eat
and blackboards bleed
and teachers skeeve at the conditions surrounding them.

I want you to get on a bus
and pass dozens of schools all close to your home.
I want your school bus to stop
20 miles out of your way at an institution they built
so you
could be with your own.

Why don't you do the things
that your ancestors made ours do?
Why don't you try living on the other side,
and then tell us that it's equal.
I want you to walk around
with the burden of knowledge that we do
and then maybe
you can tell us
racism and hatred are a thing of the past
and no longer today's issue.

With My Deepest Appreciation

For burning off more calories in a day
than you were ever allowed to eat.
For working through sun stroke
and befriending the sweltering heat.
For the gash in your head
that should have killed you,
yet you stayed planted on your feet.
For the sorrow
that should have broken you,
yet you never cried defeat.

For the little boy you carried/
never got to witness become a man.
For the little girl you birthed—
but watched disciplined by another's hand.
For the years of lost lineage
and forgotten traditions,
For the houses you built
but never lived in.
For the food you prepared
but never got to eat,
For the shoes you polished
whilst walking with bare feet.

For every tear you shed at night,
For every day you toiled.
For every pathway you shed light,
For each bit of earth your blood soiled.
For every welt…
Every burn,
Every scar

And *every* bruise…
For everything/everything—

I Thank You.

The Superior Sex

You weren't there, I reached, but you weren't there when the
lights went out,
you didn't stop to help me mend my broken wing.
You didn't sit down when the music stopped,
you didn't stay up to stoke the fire's flame.
Where were you when the ground began to shake,
who sheltered you from the rain?
What lay in your horizon when the sky began to fall,
How—
How is it from valor you abstain?

I felt my way through the darkness,
I soared above obstacles with clipped wings.
I was scorched by the fire,
but from its flames…I grew strength.
I built a mansion out of rubble,
I've found I do my best thinking on long walks in the rain.
I am the watchtower with my eye on the skyline,
a guiding post, a port in every storm, a haven—

I am necessary, I am essential,
I am from whence you came.
I am key to survival,
I am Woman
and long may I reign.

Wrongful Death

How do you quantify a life/
with dollars and cents.
How do you rectify
a wrongful death/
instituting a cash advance.
How do you tell a mother,
that it's time to say
Goodbye?
That— their child has already let go…
it's the machines
keeping them alive.
What is the cost of living,
is that price equivalent to life?
Acknowledging a wrong-doing
still doesn't make it right.
How much is one person worth,
is there a pre-established price?
What's the ball park average—
For a terminated life?

Hush Little Baby

Born with the world at your feet
so many possible things you could be.
With eyes full of wonder
and heads full of dreams.
You are our second chance
you are all we could hope to be,

Perfection that's come wrapped
in blankets of pink and blue.
Tucked in infinite possibilities
rocked in imagination…
and then we ruin you.

We teach you loathing
and we teach you fear.
You carry our resentments
and you harbor our ill will.
We teach you pain
and we teach you strife.
We give you graphic illustration
of how to devalue life.
You were perfect
and you were precious
your childish carelessness made you *great*.
We created you,
then we ruined you,
when we taught you how to hate.

The Things They Carry

These self-proclaimed warriors
These *soldiers* of our time.
Their code of conduct is unnerving
Depraved indifference is their paradigm.

They carry anger
And self-indulgence, self-entitlement and undue rage.
They climb over the weak
Trample the weary, run down the humble and humane.

Their movements—malice intent without purpose
Unable to make distinction between a hustle and a grind.
Their fight is endless
Without valor, the wreckage vast
And leaving insurmountable causalities behind.

We wade through their carnage
They prey on our fears.
We bear the burden of their namesakes
Their fight is ruthless and insincere.

Imprudent motivation
Insolvent declarations
Ill-conceived gratification
Still so much at stake left to lose.
Unfazed by anguish
Unimpressed with the truth
Unfiltered degradation
These uninspired youths.

These ruffians
These hooligans
These—*soldiers* without cause.
They've hallowed our hearts
They've broken our spirits
They're making monsters of us all.

Modern Technology

Today I skipped the news,
heard nothing old
learned nothing new.
Today I sat in contentment
with what I knew.

No typing.
No skyping.
No phones or internet.
Today I reintroduced myself to the world
as if we'd never met.

Today was such a beautiful day
there really is something to simplicity.
Today I saw the world with new eyes
and found with them God's great mercy.

The majesty of it all
is often lost on those with too much.
When you strip down to just the basics
you'll find that it's just enough.
Yet the human race continues to strive for more
of what they can do without.
Things they've never seen or heard
they act as if they can't live without.
Today I recalled the days
when my cell phone was a yell down the street.
I always heard it
the reception was always clear
Never a need to repeat.

Bittersweet memories of when I was small
Make me see
The *haves* of today
Don't really have anything at all.

Generation Y (WHY?)

I look to you
and I am saddened.
They did/so you could/and you're not.

You're angry and indignant,
they were hopeless yet sang through it.
You mock their struggle and their likeness,
but they gave their lives so you could triumph.
Creativity lays in the names you give your children
pride lies in the names you don't remember.
You don't know where you're going or what you want,
because you don't know who you are and how far we've come.

Your journey has no destination,
freedom was their manifestation.
You choose paths without purpose
and they lead to dead end streets.
They walked roads of redemption
from freedom, to equality— all in search of peace.

Tell me where you're going
and what fires light your way.
I want to hold your anger in my hands
I want to share my faith.
This is not our destination,
of this I'm sure it cannot be.
You need some more direction,
before you can live their dream.

Blessed Be

In the name of all that is *Holy*
we sail sea to shining sea.
Out of rage and retribution,
and at times– envy.

We defend our version
of what is right at all cost.
We hammer down our values
despite whatever the loss.
We storm beaches
and pitch tents in dessert sands; in defense/offense of our
freedom
on someone else's land.

Millions have been lost
and martyred for their courage.
To take a life in defense of life
is truly, truly heroic.

We do this to pay homage to you,
a token of our appreciation.
We owe you so much
we thought blood the only appropriate reparation.
We wage wars
in the name of religion/spirituality.
We rejoice in our opponents defeat.
We exhale,
We cry out
Glory!
Praises be—
To the Prince of Peace.

Dirty Word

I wanna talk about the ability
to be the better man,
To be greater than your circumstance.
To find something
in your pocketful of nothing,
then give it to someone who has less.

To stand in the midst of a storm.
and bring someone safely home.
Move a mountain
to let the sun shine on someone else's face.
Carry your brother on your back
to help him finish the race.

Go bald—
so a little girl you'll never meet
can know the joy of putting barrettes in her hair.

Turn one dollar into one hundred,
then give ninety-nine of them away.
Pray for those you've never met
to experience brighter days.

Be braver than your fear of losing
Give more than what you earn.
Do more than what's expected
Realize
Sacrifice
Is <u>not</u> a bad word.

Brown v. Board of Education

When he took on this mammoth sized fight
I don't think his vision included
Chalk outlines
And police tape.
Gang activity and stairwell rapes.

I don't think what he fought for
Was interracial bathrooms
Where everyone could gather during class.
I don't think he fought for the right
For black youths to be able to
Walk down the hall and sell some white kid
A bag of hash.

I don't think his fight included
The right for teachers to get lazy.
To have illicit affairs with students
And run off and have their babies.

I don't think he fought
For the right for history
To be forgotten.
The right to get by learning lies,
Filling children's minds with a story-teller's concoction.

I think his vision included
Us appreciating his fight.
Learning our own worth
And holding our heads up with pride.

I think he expected great things from us
When he eased the nation's subjugation.
But what we have now, is not what he envisioned then
When Brown took on the Board of Education.

Dark Child

I love latkes
and brie.
Beef bourguignon
and Irish breakfast tea.

They call me *bougie*
and of my lifestyle make jokes.
They say I'm *uppity*
and my *black card* needs to be revoked.

They—whose black history education
is isolated to calendar dates.
They—who don't know the names
of the many who are so worthy of praise.
They—who let pop culture
constrict who they are meant to be.
They—who know nothing
of the core of my identity.

I am a daughter
from a long line of single mothers
who could write anthologies on how to sacrifice.
Educate you on where you came from
and give you the tools you need to make it in life.
I am the descendant of women
who didn't know how to quit.
Who bore half a dozen children and more
and still took strangers in.

Women who smiled through their struggles
and taught me how to grind.
Who were proud of the lives they led
but for me—they wanted more for mine.
These women who taught me about the
Mohegan in me.
The Italian—
The American—
As well as my slave ancestry.

I grew up in a home
founded on hard work and integrity.
Where we listened to Sam Cooke
and Elvis Pressley.
Where we ate collard greens
and black eye peas.
Baked Challah bread
and Italian ziti.
Where you went to school
or you got a job.
Where you might not have had much
but you always had love.

I like imported vodka and single malt scotch.
Crazy Horse, Old E *AND* Sauvignon Blanc.
I like grits and cheese and grease biscuits.
Beef Wellington and mid rare steak… bone in.

This is not a fucking tan
This is who I am.
Daughter of Phillis, granddaughter of Charlotte
and all the *Phenomenal* women before them.

They gave me confidence
and taught me self-worth.
They taught me humility
and the value of hard work.
They taught me tolerance
and to appreciate creativity.
They educated me in acceptance
and the art of civility.
Their hands—the color of
chestnut, olives, peach, sandalwood and mahogany.
Their hearts—enormous, giving and unconditionally forgiving.
Their backs—strong, dependable, sturdy
and how I made it this far in life.
How dare *you* try and shame *me*
when it's you who has no pride.

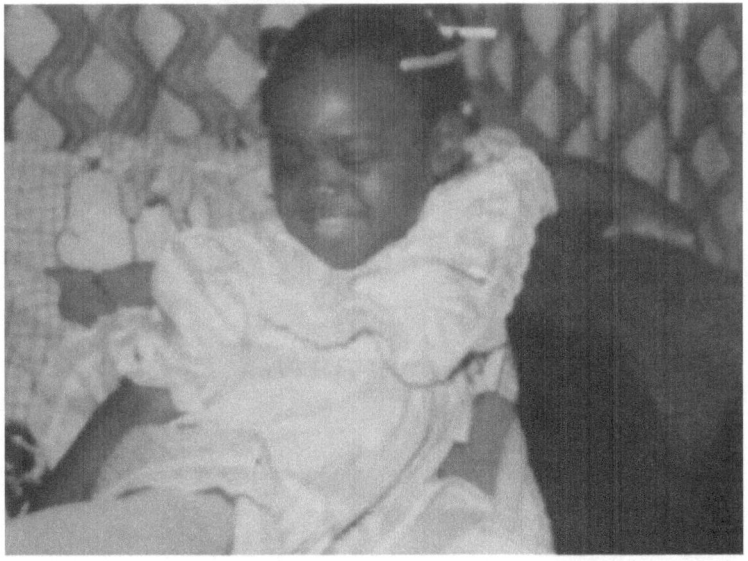

Hoodies Up

This trial will be our testament,
these tears will illustrate our rage.
This verdict a gathering storm
to the child it betrayed.
This case brought back memories
of strange fruit hanging from southern trees.
The faint scent of burning
embers clouding the Mississippi.
The winds blew in the soft
sound of four little girl's voices,
gentle cries you could barely hear.
Then came the sound of a grown man calling out,
and it echoed like a car motor in the air.

The bang of the gavel
fell down as hard as a night stick—
far too many know its sting.
Progress has brought us to an age of disparity;
It's conviction of guilt by walking.

He didn't walk far enough
we haven't come far enough
we're not quite there
yet— we're in a better place.
We've still got mountains to climb...
Sadly it's the children who are dying while we continue the race.

Evolution

My heart breaks
for the youth of today,
somewhere along the years,
society lost its way.
Trust, compassion and sacrifice,
they've become terms and ideas
instead of a way of life.

Things have gotten turned upside down
ideals, words, and culture twisted.
When did forgiving someone become so hard?
The pain used to lay in the need to ask to be forgiven.
The beauty of doing nothing
has now become known as lazy.
Today's *accidents* and *special circumstances*
were once blessings we called babies.

The identity I claim
lies in my last name
my pride and self-worth come from family.
Now the children of today
seem to all belong to gangs
brother turned against brother; everyone's an enemy.
Always being amongst the ones I love
being happy, safe and healthy was my greatest wish.
Now it's all about
popularity, unearned respect, fear, and getting rich.

I don't remember
my younger self
being surrounded by such misery.
It really makes you question life
and exactly who we are
Evolving to be.

Dysphoria

First comes the clouds
A sign the rain
Is on its way.

You can hear the thunder
See the lightening
Smell the dampness in the air.

Then it starts to drizzle
next comes the downpour
and finally you're caught in the storm.
And you're cold
And you're wet
And you're tired
And confused
And you don't know where to run.
And you're caught/caught in the rain
And you're soaked.
And then… you start to laugh
And you laugh
And laugh—and laugh.
And then… you stop
Laughing
Because you realize
That—
This is your life.
And then it's not so funny anymore.

Different

Stand for something
Pray for someone
Love ferociously
Live courageously
Dream vastly
Wish endlessly
Work diligently
Rest peacefully
Endure effortlessly
Breathe easily

Be extraordinary
And you might find your life
A little less than ordinary.

Definition

There's a word
it's not fancy
or long,
It knows little
of perfection
or overachievement.
It's quiet
and exudes an earthy ambivalence.
It's steady and soft,
it's sturdy and unyielding.
It doesn't try to posture itself to stand out
neither is it a shrinking violet
afraid of the world it's meant to flourish in.

The word is modest
and driven.
it's attentive
and caring.
It's fragile and rare
it lacks unwarranted arrogance
by sustaining ego with prayer.
The word is hopeful and humble
it's earnest and sincere.
It's awkward and majestic,
It's generous, its heart's without fear.

In a world where it's possible
to be anything you want to be.
I will stay true to my word
and all that it encompasses
and that word
is Me.

Score

Addict: I need something real bad man, I'll do anything—*please* I'm sick.

Dealer: I ain't in the business of giving handouts man, I ain't running no charity, pay up if you want your fix.

Addict: Come on, don't, *don't* me like that, you know I'm good for it, I swear.

Dealer: That's the same sad story you told last time you came begging around here.

Addict: Please—I'll do anything, just tell me what you want me to do.

Dealer: Well… I did get this new product in, I could use me a good mule.

Addict: I'm yours. Just give it to me, I need something now really bad.

Dealer: Here you go my friend; you get the first sample bag.

Addict: What is this shit!? It's amazing. I'd get more if I wasn't broke.

Dealer: This right here is that stuff from way back; the streets named it *Hope*.

Utopia

How upset can we truly be with them,
on whom does all the blame lay?
The path they've walked was laden with progressive ideology
and now everyone is paying the price.

Is it truly right to punish them,
they were only being the people they were raised to be.
They were taught to question everything,
now you want to strip them of their right to free speech.
They were never shown where the line was
or told what it might cost to cross it.
They were led to believe the world owed them something
now their sense of entitlement is wreaking havoc.

I think we may have overreached
on what we expected from the next generation.
So, take a good look around
And don't you dare cry now
This is the utopia of our own creation.

Duty Bound

Too many are ill equipped
and greatly underprepared.
Not emotionally developed enough
and operating out of fear.
Not pragmatic enough to compromise.
No vast skill set to utilize.
Not strategic enough to incentivize.
Not heroic enough to rationalize.

You were supposed to be our modern-day knights
personifying valor and chivalry.
But now there's an air of contention and distrust
as you patrol these now tumultuous streets.

I know you are only human
if cut, yes—you will bleed.
So you rally to distribute law and order
but what happened to simply maintaining the peace?

If the public you promised to serve and protect
cripples you with fear and puts you ill at ease.
Well my regrets to you, but that's a reality you should have
considered
before you decided to join the police.

Value Lost

There was a certain truth in the sweat
An honesty in the exhaustion
A sense of pride in the result; but now hard work
Means that you've worked too hard,
Caring means you're soft.
Honesty makes you a snitch
Faith makes you crazy
My God, what values we've lost.

Anywhere But Here

Sometimes I just wanna cry,
just crawl inside myself
and hide.
Just disappear
from human sight.

I feel the need to sleep.
Just close my eyes and catch a dream.

To open my eyes
and be in a different place.
Where words
only bring smiles to another's face.
Where weapons are not forged
to bring another harm.
Where children always go home
to the tenderness of their parents' arms.

I just need
to leave this place.
Go follow my heart,
feel destiny's embrace.
But first I need to go to sleep
to close my eyes and say my prayers.
to hope against hope
that when I wake
that I'm anywhere but here.

Feeling anything but loneliness,
Doing anything but nothing,
Going anywhere but staying here.
I want to wake up and be free from fear.

I want to wake up and be happy
to feel free to be who I am.
No consequences or repercussions
no ceding to another's demands.
I want to wake up in a world
where there is no hate
and all intentions are sincere.
I want wake up and be *ANYWHERE*
But here.

That Thing

It's often born in the most tumultuous of times,
it's in the blood, the sweat and the tears.
It can be found entwined in yearning
and in the most debilitating of fears.
It's often hidden in the darkness
often ripped apart by storms.
It thrives in desperation,
it's rooted in chaos and harm.
Once found it's often praised,
once developed it never fades.
Never lost,
and can't be bought.
It's vastly admired,
and highly desired…
<u>Character.</u>

The Human Experience

We all experience it...
Different versions of it.
Yet very few understand; it's incomparable,
Unintelligible—not something easily shared.
It can't be held,
Can't be touched.
It's inconsolable and uncontrollable.
You can't feel it
Unless you're in it.
It's all consuming—
It's heavy and thick
Hot and cold all over
It makes you gasp for breath.

Hurt...Can you feel it?

A New Nation Conceived In...

Because *advancement* and *progress*
now mean two entirely different things.
Because truth's become a liability
a caged bird with clipped wings.
Because humanitarians
are now on the endangered species list.
Because innocence is irrelevant
and *justice* can be purchased.

Because *The Dream*
has become a fable
a bedtime story for the kids.
Because they televised the revolution
and compromised
Intelligence.
Because he saw it for himself
and thinks the ovens were too small.
Because denial, dismissal and arrogance
are the makings of a holocaust.

Because of the doctors
who can't treat us.
Because of the preachers
who can't save us.
Because of nature
that can't restore us.
Because of the historical fiction
that they feed us.

Because of the lineage
that can't be traced.
Because of those
who kept their faith.
Because of fortitude
and determination.
Because of the calloused hands
that built a nation.

Because Sojourner spoke the truth.
Because Alex shared his roots.
Because they stood tall on Wounded Knee
Because they rejected foreign manifestation of their destiny.

Because the signs been taken down,
no more *give me your tired, your poor huddled masses yearning
to breathe free.*
Because the lamp oil's run dry
because this is not a place to seek salvation
because the signs now states *NO SOLICITING.*

Because peace seems unattainable
Because faith seems infantile
Because hope is paralyzing
Because generosity has become marginalized.
Because forgiveness became a way to capitalize.

Because I don't know what comes with
Being *great again*
What does *greatness* even mean?
Because *THE OVENS WERENT BIG ENOUGH*
Because—I'm afraid of the new regime.

I Know Not What Course...
(I hear you Sir. P Henry)

Why stand we here idle,
What has become of us?
The irons grow heavy still,
The chains are gathered in filth and rust.
Here united we lay waiting,
Silently taking it all in.
Hunkered down in inaction,
Seeing and hearing each trending devastation.

I beseech you—come out!
Please let me show you the way.
My friend Harriett has a cabin in the woods
Let her teach you of bravery.
The battle is not to the strong alone.
You must hear the story of her Uncle Tom.
I shall arrange you passage
With a dear old friend of mine.
Mrs. Cady-Stanton, she will lead the way,
She will be your guide.
The journey may be arduous
and I know not what lamp may light your path.
But fear not, a mighty Chief has left a trail of tears,
The trail will keep you right on track.
Once you've reached your destination,
And you've had your fill of thought.
There's a Horse that's running Crazy,
He will come and seek you out.
He will carry you to Boston
Where the bergamot meets the bay.

Where the sounds of indignation
Crash steadily against the waves.

A ship will charter you to Europe,
Where you will meet my dear friend Tom Paine.
He writes letters in the darkness
That speak of brighter days.
He will bring you to a meeting
Where friends of ours lay in wait.
They want to tell you stories
Of their triumphant escapades.
Ms. Sendler and Mr. Schindler
Oh what tales the two could tell.
Despite the anguish to their flesh
They've done good at keeping secrets to themselves.

Your journey will be long
And tired you may be.
But I really must insist you see Lord Mansfield,
And join him for some tea.
He has stories of his own
That tell of great intrigue.
And perhaps while you are there
You might visit with his niece.

Alas, your journey had been extended
And yet all my friends you haven't met.
They are scattered across the globe
But now your journey's come to an end.
There is so much more to tell you
All riveting, inspiring stuff.
But I see now you are ready to aid in the search for others
Who share their humanitarian lust.

There is no time for ceremony
The world has become a devastating place.
We must find more individuals like my friends
To repair that which Heaven gave.
I know there are more out there,
I found you,
So I know there is.
Take my hand
And help me search,
I beseech you, come out, come out
And show me how big your brave is.

That's How I Eat

It's that vibe
that makes you want to sweat.
Live life fearlessly
and without regret.

It's melodic perspective
that humbles you—builds and strips your pride.
Compresses that long desired exhale,
hugs that deep guttural cry.

It's lyrics that inspire sympathy.
Piano keys that rain down memories.
Vocals that you feel.
Tempos that help heal.
Bridges that repair.
A message—a statement—a promise…a prayer.

A heavy bass to help ease
life's unbearable load.
It's that universal harmony
it's music—its good food for the soul.

Here's Where I Stand

Do I contradict myself?

I don't believe in torture
but I think some people
should rot in hell.
I find a lot of times
violence unnecessary
but a firm hand is effective when used well.

I don't believe in fairytales
but I think folklore
is derived from a bit of truth.
While there's much about
history I've forgotten
I'll never forget the Golden Rules.

I have an affinity
for wild things
yet they scare me half to death.
I think the beast of the wild
while they would kill me—
are majestic and deserving of our respect.

I think babies are blessings
yet feel some should have never been born.
To create a life just for it to suffer
is sadistic and egregiously wrong.

I think education is important
but find a great number of learning institutions lacking.
I'm appalled by complacent ignorance
and find illiteracy and the inability to comprehend maddening.

I can honestly say I wish to be healthy
and I know what living a healthy lifestyle means.
While I don't use drugs, I also don't exercise
and I swear excessively as well as smoke and drink.

I want to be well read
but sometimes find reading a bit of a chore.
I find imagination the greatest of gifts
as well as a double-edged sword.
So *Yes*, I contradict myself.

I empathize with the poor
yet I don't feed them.
I love children
yet I have none.
I think money is the root of all evil
yet I go to work everyday.
I've yet to witness a miracle
but that doesn't stop me from praying.
I don't want to be fat
but I enjoy food too much to diet.
I enjoy the company of others
but I love to have peace and quiet.
I'm hopeful for a better tomorrow
but I'm terrified of what the future might bring.
By nature I'm reclusive and apprehensive
but I long to see, hear and do brave things.

So what! I contradict myself—
I know exactly who I am.
I am exactly who I was raised to be
and this is where I stand.

Love

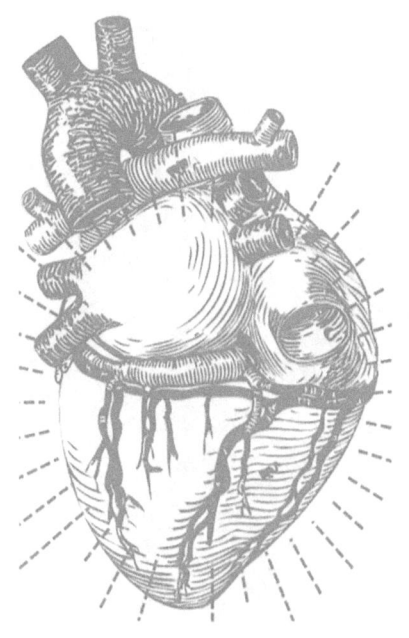

Words' Worth

You told me once you loved me,
you promised you'd never leave.
Yet I'm sending you this letter across an ocean
to a place I've never seen.
You promised me forever,
you said our wealth was copious and unseen.
You and I, we were each other's dream.

You packed your bags and left me
without the conviction to say it to my face.
You left me a letter to end it all....
Actions without grace.
You left
You ran
You left me a letter—
You didn't have the nerve to say it to my face.

Now you're sending me this letter
after years with no word from you.
You just want to start off with telling me you're sorry,
you just want me to see things from your point of view.

You want me to be understanding
You want me to search my heart.
You want me to forgive you...
After you ripped my world apart.

You say that you regret leaving
That I never left your mind.
You say that you still love me
You want to give *us* another try.

You just want the chance *you* deserve
You're just so very sorry...
I should search the pieces of my broken heart
You <u>deserve</u> a chance.
You're sorry
And I—I should understand.

My Dearest,
Yes, I understand you're sorry,
Yes, you're sorry, true indeed.
I learned a long time ago
Sorry, is the worst kind of person
one could ever hope to be.

Yes, I know you're sorry
and your word is all that you have.
But I have learned how much your word is worth
and what character you lack.

My Dearest First Love,

Separated by years and ocean,

my love for you is constant.

There is no one else who will ever love you the way I do,

there is no person in this world who can fill the void of you.

I left my heart with you

when I was just a girl.

I've shared time and space with others

but you were my fairytale.

The vision of your smile

leaves me breathless,

the memory of your embrace makes me radiate with heat.

It doesn't seem right to let someone else love me

when you never gave my heart back to me.

You're gone and you're not coming back

of this I am quite sure.

But could you send me back the love I gave you

because I haven't anymore.

-Eternally Yours

Match dot Com

What are you looking for?

Humility; and the sincerity that comes with it, the tenderness that stems from it, and the warmth that emanates from it.

Integrity; and the loyalty that often follows, the stability through life's trials and the faith that offers solace.

Strength; and the clarity that comes with it, the knowledge that it's not hidden in a balled fist and the courage it takes to lend it.

I want valor.
I want someone to breathe life back into chivalry.
Hold my hand through adversity;
Share in all my victories…
Marvel in all that is me.

SEARCH

Noli Me Tangere

I left it in the corner
On the floor
In the dark
In the far back corner
That's
Where I left it.

Keep it safe for me.
Hide it
Where no one else can see.
Protect it from the elements
for it's all that's left of me.
I'm entrusting it to you
because you're everything to me.

I'm leaving you, my heart.

Sacrifice

A fistful of tears
The weight of my heart
The purity of my soul
The gleam in my eye
The brilliance of my mind.

I'd give it all—

No price too high.
To never have to hear you
Ever say goodbye.

Have a Little Faith in Me

Trust who I am,
See hope in my eyes.
Feel compassion in my touch,
Find light in my smile.
Know that I will make wrong turns,
Have bad judgment,
And cover up mistakes I don't want you to see.
But listen to your heart, look deep within my soul,
Know that I Will Be Okay,
Just— have a little faith in me.

Adièu

I cannot talk to sorrow
she cannot be reasoned with.
She is cold
and she is hollow
And her temper—unforgiving.

She stalks me night and day,
she plagues me with misdirection.
Unyielding in her pursuits,
countless late-night indiscretions.

I've tried to drown her with spirits
Used love to counter her ambivalence
But she is witty and unrelenting
She knows nothing of forgiveness.

She is bold and she is callous.
Mother of hate and mistress of malice.
Her weight is dense and hefty—
cumbersome enough to bring one to their knees.
She is irrational
and she is merciless
and she… will be the death of me.

Ache

Dearest Heart,

I couldn't sleep
a wink last night,
still, I laid with bated breath.
Mind paralyzed,
Body traumatized,
I command you
Let me rest.

I cannot breathe
I cannot eat
I cannot be—without him.
Be still,
Be still! My beating heart,
How dare you
Beat without him.

I Call your Bluff

It's getting late in the game
so this is the last hand.
So as the cards are dealt,
I'll let you know exactly where I stand.

I know inside you're hurting
and no words can ease your pain.
Although others have dwelt along your path,
their experience was not the same.
And although with all my heart,
I Love You,
your *sorrys* and excuses are just that.
Sorry attempts to excuse your lies
and to hide your dirty past.

I don't pretend to know
the hand in life you hold.
But it really doesn't matter,
life has dealt me a hand of my own.

Though others may try and play your hand
for you,
for my sake
and yours alone.
I'm laying down my cards,
so either you come see me…
or choose to fold.

L'amore E Cieco

I almost forgot
What you
Loving me
Felt like.

Your love is like
dozens of broken bones
piercing arteries and organs.
Your love is like
the inability to tread water
and being dropped in the middle of the ocean.
Your love is like a wildfire
in the middle of a heatwave.
Your love is like a plane crashing
just miles from hitting the run-way.

I'd almost forgotten
How I felt
When I let you love me.

It felt like trying to breathe
through a coffee straw.
It felt like sitting passenger seat in a vehicle
and heading high speed at a wall.
It felt like walking a mile
in sneakers filled with glass.
It felt like being diagnosed with a terminal disease
that was advancing way too fast.

I had almost forgot
What it felt like
When you loved me
And I missed you
But then you called.
And in the midst
Of my excitement
My mind flashed back to memories of it all.

Your love is cold
and it hurts.
Your love is too intense
and I was often left burned.
You have no idea how much it kills me
to hear you say those three little words.

You called…
And for a second I forgot
How it felt—
I forgot, and then you called.
But then I remembered, I remembered
How much it hurt/being loved by you
is one of the most painful things of all.

I Gave Up

I didn't find it
when I sought it out,
I looked for it everywhere
searched high and low.
Turned over every rock and boulder,
still I came up empty each time/
walked away with nothing to show.
I held my breath
to hear it better,
but the silence got too loud.
I closed my eyes and tried to sense it,
but got lost in the darkness that I found.
I walked aimlessly for miles
hoping it would bump into me,
but never did it cross my path.
So, I retreated from my mission
and suddenly, love found me at last.

To The Man I Haven't Met... Yet

I give you me.
I give you all my hopes, fears, aspirations
and insecurities.
I give you my heart,
my soul,
my tears,
my faith.
I give you my compassion,
my forgiveness
for your every and any mistake.

I promise you my breath
when it seems you'll drown in sorrow.
I promise you my sight
when you can't see clearly to tomorrow.
I promise you my *will*
for whatever storms you might go through.

I promise you my hand
if ever your road not be lit.
I promise you my drive
Should you ever find yourself wanting to quit.
I promise
though death might part us
in my spirit
You will remain ever present.
I promise—
To
Love
Honor
And Cherish.

Love's a Funny Thing

Quite carelessly I fell in love
I ran from it for quite a while.
Its exquisite pain
Its deplorable torture
Its inexplicable need to devour.

Quite earnestly I made my case
that love was not for me.
Its desperate longing
Its tireless sorrow
Its constant need—its greed.

Quite by coincidence you found me hiding
I was the *nobody* you singled out
I saw you when I wasn't looking
Not quite lost but all the same… I was found.

Quite foolishly I fell for you
Gave you the best of me.
I lost my heart
Surrendered all—
Then watched you take your leave.

To The Shepherd From His Love
(With Marlowe in mind)

I should have run away with you
I should have left it all and run away.
I see now what my hesitation has earned me
I see now what it cost to stay.

A simple life atop a hill.
With flower beds
And golden field.
These things you offered—
But I wanted more.
I have them now,
But I'd surrender them all.
To be with you—
And be your love.

Just One Forever

Something soft and gentle,
like a cool steady breeze in May.
Something as strong as a diamond,
a glimmering brilliance that will never know decay.
Something as steady as a pendulum,
a constant beat that never fades.
Something as epic as a fairytale,
that transcends time, gender and age.
Something endless like forever,
always given but can never truly be attained.
Something captivating like a spirit,
never seen but always praised.

I want a love like that.

I want to be offered forever
and given eternity.
I want your heart and soul
to want to write and sing a song for me.
I want your heart
to beat with mine.
I want a romance to inspire fables
a tale that withstands the test of time.

Give me the impossible
Wrap me in the intangible
Lead me to the unimaginable.

Love me
Unconditionally.

Anorexia

I want to feel...
your breath on my neck,
your chest on my back,
the beat of your heart,
and your arms holding me.

Instead...

I feel...
The pain of my ribs,
the rumble of my stomach,
the faint thump of my pulse
and an intuition
that has turned on me.

I feel starved for attention,
I hunger for affection.
My heart's been beaten
into submission,
and I ache for some protection.

I need love and commitment.
Faith and fulfillment.
I want to live life
with joy and laughter.
I want to find my soul-mate
and live happily ever after.

My mind, body and soul are yearning
for someone
to feed me.

All Dressed Up In Love

A weathered jacket,
A fuzz filled scarf.
Some sole-less shoes,
A shawl ravaged by moths.
Some well-worn slacks,
And a holey shirt.
Some mismatched socks,
And a woolen cap caked in dirt.
Middle of winter,
Snow at my waist.
But I'm warmer than ever,
Praises be to love's embrace.

Love Me Long Time

I don't want to settle
I don't want everything
to just be *okay*.
I'd much rather fall…
I'm okay with the pain.

A courageous heart
can be a deadly thing.
It gives
and it takes
it devours—and it redeems.

I want a love
that is caution-less.
Disrespectful—
and relentless.
I want love
to make a mess of me.
Cut me deep
then watch me bleed.
Pick me up
then throw me down.
A careless love
that flings me around.
A love not afraid
to show its teeth.
Bare it all
and leave me weak.

I want to fall
I want to plunge
I want to crash
right into love.
Hurt me
Hold me
Catch me
Show me what your love's made of.

Give me love.
Let me fall.

For What Ails You

My misery found company with you
long sleepless restless nights
you made me feel so good.
Tossing and turning
sweating and moaning.
Slow heavy stroking
drunk love, sobered by morning.

I'm not ashamed of what I had to do.
Convinced myself that I might just love you
reasoned all the shame away
prayed for day to go away
and night to bring me back to you.

Insanity had me by the throat.
Twisted in madness I felt out of control.
The scent of lust that fills the air.
The way you grab at my hair.
The weight of your body on top of mine.
The racing of my heart, the strength in your arms.
Everything's that's been wrong.
Is gone in the dark.

The Vow

The sound of slow shuffling feet,
the smell of sweat and musk.
The weary grin of satisfaction,
the calloused feel of your touch.
The dependability of your presence,
the integrity of your work.
The sincerity in every word you speak,
your esteem for what life's worth.

Without a penny to your name
Without a single inch of land.
Without any higher education
Without authority to command.

I will love you.

Passion

I'm looking for
The infinite possibility
To have anything.
The probability
Of self-contentment.
The assumption
That…
There is still good out there.

I'm looking for
Beauty,
Non-diminishing.
Age—
Not prohibiting.
Love
Everlasting.
I'm looking for
Hope
And compassion.

I'm looking for a reason to live.

Faith

Thou Shalt Not

When judgement day
comes rolling in
and of your life
you must recount.
What testimony
will you give,
what poignancy stands out?

I've seen you march
and I've heard you chant
and to me, you seem quite proud.
But will that change
on judgement day
when you confess in your final hour?

Of what I know
of the God you serve
he sounds a lot like mine.
He who wept in
in the face of hate
would be shattered by the atrocities of our time.

No doctrine
teaches war,
no faith
manifests hate.
No scripture
incites violence
no *prophet* hides behind faith.

All in life is fleeting
all that's fought for
will be lost.
You cannot take it with you
yet you fight to hold on to what you have
at a devastating cost.
Your claims of racial superiority
your declaration of blood purity
they carry absolutely no currency.
In the end…
You're just as dead
just as buried
as those you deemed unworthy.

In the end
what will you say
to *He* who gave his life?
What will your explanation be
When he ask…
Who gave you the right?

You Found Who? Where?

I have scoured the globe,
I have searched high and low.
From the beaches in Fiji
to the Victorian falls.
Climbed the pyramids in Egypt
I've scoured the ruins in Rome.
I've trekked through Brazilian jungle
searched every inch of the Parthenon.

I've seen waters so blue
the horizon couldn't separate them from the sky.
I've seen sunsets so glorious
that even the shadows looked divine.

I saw him in a starry night
I saw him in the sea.
I saw him on a mountain top
I saw him blowing in the breeze.

You don't have to be lost to find him,
you don't have to be down on your luck.
You don't have to go to prison to find him
Believe me—
Christ… Is not locked up.

Life

He created Hope
For the hopeless
Mercy for those who don't deserve it
Peace for those who won't find it
And Prayer for those who won't use it.

Compassion to generate kindness
Mercy to inspire
Redemption to revive
And Faith for peace of mind.

He wants us all to
Love without fear
Trust without reason
Hope without limit
Wonder without speculation.

Just live.

Dear Atheist,

If not for the promise of better days
if not for the light
and his way.
If not for the love
and the strength in his name,
there'd be no cause for today.

To look at the world
and think this is it,
and think it's not all part of a plan.
Must be draining and sad
and hard to go on,
never knowing it is all in his hands.

To never know love
like that, that he gave
when he carried the cross
for our souls.
Puts you at a disadvantage in life,
for how could you give what you've never known.

I can't understand how you can live
and think the world of flesh is the end,
and doubt his mercy divine.
For when my days are done on this earth,
it pleases my heart to know
that I'll see my family and friends once again, and
Oh!
What a Time, What A Time!

I can see you in your final hour
terrified,
desperately hanging on,
Scared to let go.
Not having the peace of mind or the joy that it brings
to be able to say,
It is well, *It Is Well*, with my soul.

The Right To Decide

Somewhere deep
within the storm of insincerity
twisted within people's frailties
bound by propaganda,
lost in the world's scandals—
there lies a tiny cry,
an overlooked pair of
sad tiny eyes.
There lies a neglected and moaning tummy—
a bruised heart
that's oh, so lonely.
There lies
What is right,
There lies
What is light
There lies
A tiny forgotten life.

Too many times
born into a world so wanton,
born to adults
maturity has forgotten.
Thrown into a place
where only the brave go.
This space/place…The abyss we call—
Ghetto.

Here there is no time
for tears.
Here lies the origin
of most people's fears.

Here happiness reigns
on no one's face.
Here the educated
are out of place.
Here where a pipe
is your haven.
Here where silence
is a cry for salvation.

This is where our children live
This is where
They roam the streets.
This is where their souls
Cry out,
This is there they learn
Defeat.

Opposite this place of terror
lies another wanton place.
This place that they call
Milk and *Honey*
hides their betrayals and disgrace.
They hide behind their PhD's,
their charge accounts and family crest.
Behind closed doors
They yell and scream,
they only think
they're better than the rest.

They primp, they press
their needles erase life's lines.
They laugh and play and ski and drink
and at night their children silently cry.

They haven't the time for skinned knees
and bruised hearts.
They don't juggle their schedules
to talk or to read,
inside their home lives a family apart.

There lies no difference
between the rich and the poor
when it comes to neglecting their children.
The surroundings may be something quite different
but all the same emotions still fill them.
The hate and the yearning, the fear and the loneliness,
the despair and the idolatry—
The feeling of loss and apathy.

These poor souls serve as proof
That
God doesn't always look after
Babies and fools.
So Heaven help us,
And God have mercy
If we ever loose
Our right to choose.

I Beg Your Pardon

They say that they are your sheep
but
they don't follow you.
They say they are devout,
But they don't walk the roads you choose.

They say they've been saved
By the institutions they've built for you.
They throw money to pay penance
For the injustices they do.

They do not cover the cold
Or visit the sick.
They do not comfort the lonely
Or take the stranger in.

But when in distress
Or a time of great need.
They fall to their knees and cry out your name
And beg of your pardon please.

Family

I've never seen
such a weak foundation.
I feel burdened with the weight
of previous generations.
So many skeletons
should never see the light of day.
How much heartache
can one person take?
Lied to directly
and beaten with guilt.
Tormented by blood
but a connection never felt.
A loyalty never earned
and a bond that's half baked.
Cold and callous manipulation
and an endearment so fake.
Brought together
by a significant commonality.
Please—
God forgive me
If I do not love my family.

Smiling With My Eyes Closed

I can hear you laughing
when I close my eyes.
I'll always remember
everything you taught me
and every tear you dried.

Precious memories of your love
have yet to age a day.
The terms of your endearment,
how you did it all—
your way.

You've left footprints on my heart
no other shoes can fill
your love is what makes me whole.
And I'll never forget
how good it felt
as I watched you, watch me
grow old.

Old Time Religion

Give me that old time religion
Talkin' 'bout religion, *good* religion
Like it used to be.
That religion that had me kneeling
At the altar each Sunday,
The church's praise that brought me to my feet.
That religion that saw you through
Each and every week.
That religion that helped you care
For your neighbor down the street.
That old time religion Lord,
Hallelujah!
It was good enough for me.

Give me that old time religion
The one with vacation bible school,
And bible study and prayer lists;
That religion that went outside of the church/
Into your home,
Fund-raised you a way to eat, and prayed
You a bed where you could sleep.
That religion that kept a watchful eye
When your babies were out of arm's reach.
That old time religion Lord,
Hallelujah!
It was good enough for me.

It was good for my dear old Grandmother
She who tithed from home
Each and every week.
She who fish-fried for the choir,

and dinner plated for the retreat.
She who gave me change every Sunday,
For my own offering Lord.
It was good enough for her...
Hallelujah—
It's good enough for me.

Give me that old time religion,
Talkin' 'bout religion, *good* religion like it used to be.
That religion that held me through the hurt,
Pushed me nearer to the cross;
Helped me make amends with God,
That kept the altar candles lit for me
Whenever I got lost.
That religion that I saw love people through
Their darkest days
And loneliest nights;
That religion that gave them the faith and understanding
To know that in the end it would all be alright.
That religion full of joy and praise and hope,
That religion that offered a sense of peace.
That old time religion Lord,
Hallelujah!
Good Enough For Me!

Walk By Faith, Not By Sight

The cries were as loud
as thunder
they echoed in my ears.
I heard allegations of desertion
saw crying faces with no tears.
Steel soared across the earth
like lightning,
splintering family and faith.
Hopelessness clouded the sky
and then…
then came the rain.

The rage and despair
that poured down
was enough
to drown a nation.
Rumors denying your existence
spread to every region/hatred flourished
all to *He* who had "forsaken."

Then…

I felt your heartache
In earthquakes,
Felt your tears
In every storm.
Heard your call
In every wind blow
Saw your hope
In every dawn.

Cross My Heart and Hope To Die

I've never understood the pursuit
of the fountain of youth.
Why people choose immortality
and hide from life's one ultimate truth.

I think death is a state of clarity

To live forever...
what does that mean?
eventually won't you stop living anyway,
won't life just become a way of being?
To watch everyone you love
grow old and pass away.
Just leaving you behind
To exist another day.

Life is a beautiful struggle
a glistening ripple in time.
Don't run from all that's waiting for you
beyond the great divide.

Pass Me Not

Pass me not, *O Gentle Savior*
Amongst the huddled masses
Here I stand.
On my faith,
On the strength of your word…
Come find me, here I am.

Hear my humble cry.

In my darkest hours
My will forgone
It's your name that I call…

Don't pass me by.

Mine is but one voice
Trying to soar above gunfire, sirens and screams.
I'm in need of you, Savior
In need of saving.
I come to you humbly. Do not pass me.

Please don't pass—
Please don't pass me by.

Until Angels Close My Eyes

Given the chance to do it all again
I'd kindly decline the offer.
The chance to somehow live again
is something I'd never go after.
Life is the most precious gift
one could ever have.
For some life seems like a punishment/
a chance they never had.

It is the most beautiful
destruction you'd ever see.
The happiest hurt
you'd ever feel.

Wonderful memories made
to be forgotten.
Bonds forged
to be broken.
Hope inspired
to be forsaken.
Faith established
and often shaken.

I gladly take part in all of it
and do my best
to push sorrow aside.
I'll enjoy each fleeting
moment of it
until angels close my eyes.

www.ingramcontent.com/pod-product-compliance
Lightning Source LLC
Chambersburg PA
CBHW031441120626
46545CB00006B/2511